BEFORE YOU BEGIN...

Make sure to download the FREE audio program for this book which comes with your purchase! Just go to

www.slangman.com/audio

then look for your book and enter this code:

E2F25I2QB6PL

GOLDILOCKS
and the 3 BEARS

Book Design
and Production:
Slangman Publishing.

Written by: David Burke
Copy Editor: Julie Bobrick
Illustrated by: "Migs!" Sandoval
Translator: David Burke
Proofreader: Emmanuelle Rousseaux

Copyright © 2017 by David Burke

Email: info@heywordy.com
Website: www.heywordy.com

Hey Wordy! and all related characters and elements
are © and trademarks of Hey Wordy, LLC.

Published by Slangman Publishing. Slangman is a registered trademark of David Burke. All rights reserved. Reproduction or translation of any part of this work beyond that permitted by section 107 or 108 of the 1976 United States Copyright Act without the permission of the copyright owner is unlawful. Requests for permission or further information should be addressed to the Permissions Department, Slangman Publishing. This publication is designed to provide accurate and authoritative information in regard to the subject matter covered. The persons, entities and events in this book are fictitious. Any similarities with actual persons or entities, past and present, are purely coincidental.

ISBN13: 978-1-891888-13-7

Printed in the U.S.A.

Meet the Author
David Burke

Creator and star of the children's TV show, *Hey Wordy!*, David Burke has been single-handedly revolutionizing the foreign language-learning movement worldwide.

In addition to being a performer of boundless energy and enthusiasm, David speaks seven languages. A successful author and entrepreneur, he has built a thriving international publishing company featuring over 100 books he has written for teen/adults & children. His books have won publishing awards and have sold more than one million copies. David's Street Speak™ and Biz Speak™ series of books and audio programs are used around the world by government agencies, leading universities and major corporations.

Since age 4, David has been a classically trained pianist and uses his musical gifts to compose and perform original songs for his TV series, *Hey Wordy!* which introduces children to foreign languages and cultures through music, animation, and magical adventures. He has also composed, orchestrated, and performed all the music in the audio programs for each of these books.

David's engaging and charismatic persona became a fixture on broadcast entertainment channels around the world, such as CNN and the BBC. David and his work have been highlighted in many major publications, including The Los Angeles Times, The Chicago Tribune and The Christian Science Monitor.

"This series teaches everyday words that occur in your child's life, as well as terms having to do with politeness, greetings, family & friendship."

David Burke

French vocabulary taught:

bébé = baby
bol = bowl
chaud = hot
cuisine = kitchen
deux = two
dur = hard
fatiguée = tired
fauteuil = armchair
froid = cold
lit = bed

maman = mama
mou = soft
ours = bear
papa = papa
petit = little
porte = door
promenade = stroll
table = table
trois = three
un = one

from Cindellera (Level 1)

amoureux = in love
au revoir = goodbye
beau = handsome
belle = pretty
chaussure = shoe
de rien = you're welcome
épouse = wife
fête = party
fille = girl
grande = big

heureuse = happy
maison = house
méchante = mean
merci = thank you
minuit = midnight
moment = moment
pied = foot
prince = prince
robe = dress
triste = sad

1

ours ←

papa ←

maman ←

Once upon a time, there was a bear family who lived in a *grande maison* in the forest — a papa ours, a very loving mama, and their pride and joy,

a (little) (baby) **ours**. The **petit bébé ours** was very *beau* like his **papa**. The **papa ours** was very much *amoureux* with the loving **maman** and they were so

→ **petit**

→ **bébé**

3

proud of their family. One day, the **maman** prepared some soup for lunch, but it was too hot. While it cooled off, the **ours** family decided to take a stroll.

promenade

Meanwhile in a town nearby, there lived a **belle fille** named Goldilocks who was very **triste** because she was so tired of never having anything fun to do.

5

She thought for one **moment** and decided to take a **promenade** in the forest. Very soon, she came upon a **maison** and knocked on the door but no one

porte ←

was there. So she opened the **porte**, put one *pied* inside the *maison*, and said "Hello? Is anyone home?" She was very ⟨tired⟩ after her long **promenade** → **fatiguée**

and since no one answered, she walked inside the *maison*. She looked around for a *moment* and was very *heureuse* to see a table in the kitchen with food

table ←
cuisine ←

8

on it! She quickly approached the **table** in the **cuisine** and was super extra *heureuse* because there on the **table** in the **cuisine** was a bowl — **bol**

9

un
deux
trois

but not just one **bol**, not just two **bols**, but three **bols**! **Un, deux, trois! Trois bols** of something that smelled wonderful! She took a taste from the **bol** of the

papa ours and said, "Oh! This is too [hot]!" → **chaud**
Then she took a taste from the **bol** that
belonged to the **maman** and said, "Oh!
This is too [cold]!" Then she took a taste → **froid**

from the **petit bol** and said, "Ahhhhh. This one isn't too **chaud**. It isn't too **froid**. It's just right!" And she ate everything in the **petit bol**. "*Merci!*" she said to the empty

petit bol. Well, now she was even more **fatiguée** than ever after eating so much food. So, she decided to rest. In the living room, she saw an armchair...but not just

fauteuil

13

un fauteuil, not just **deux fauteuils**, but **trois fauteuils**! **Un**, **deux**, **trois**! **Trois fauteuils**! So, she sat down in the **fauteuil** of the **papa ours** and said,

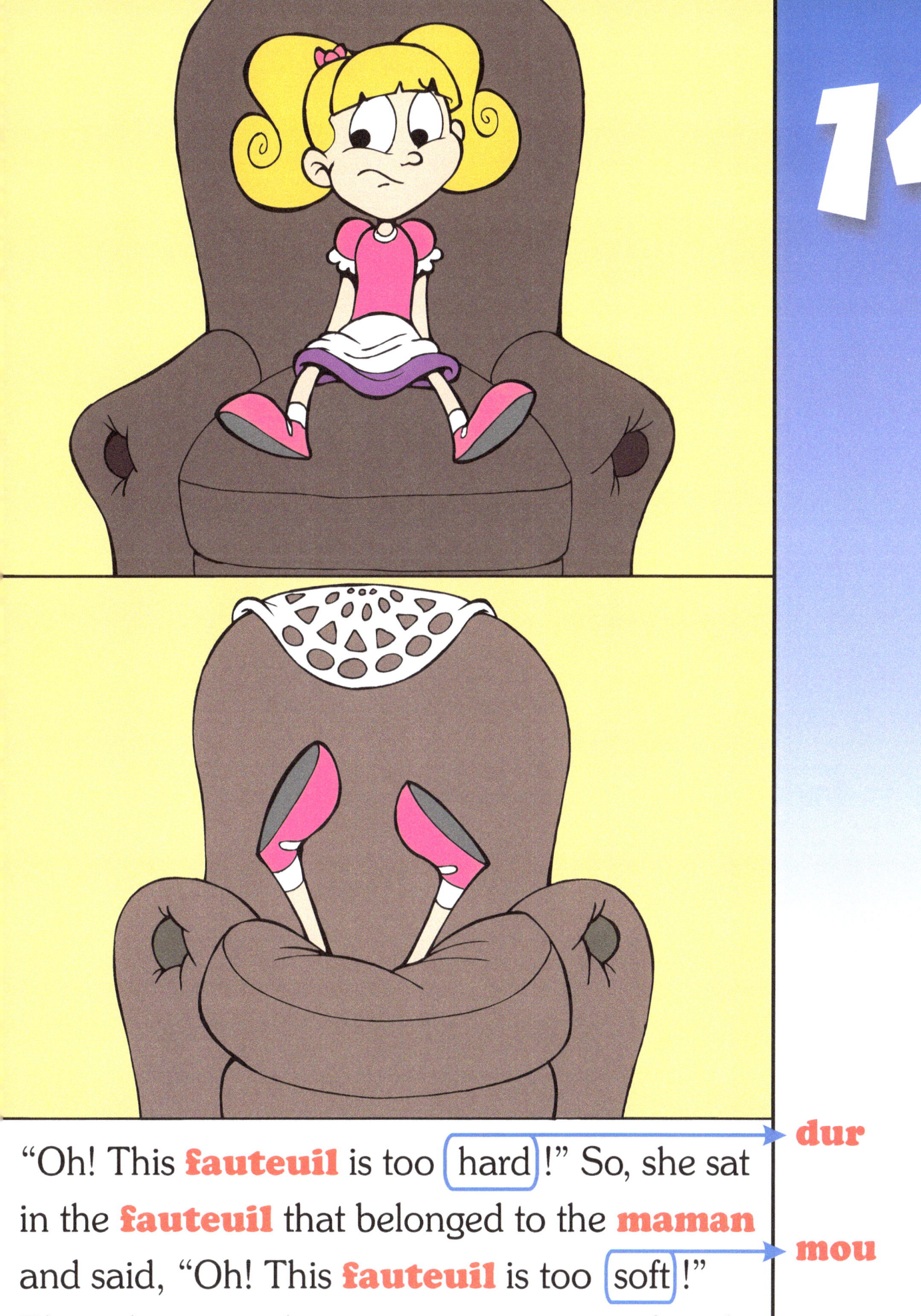

"Oh! This **fauteuil** is too hard !" → **dur**
So, she sat in the **fauteuil** that belonged to the **maman** and said, "Oh! This **fauteuil** is too soft !" → **mou**
Then she sat in the **petit fauteuil** and said,

15

"Ahhhhh. This one isn't too **dur**. It isn't too **mou**. It's just right!" But just as she got comfortable... *Crack!* The **petit fauteuil** completely fell apart! Still **fatiguée** from

her **promenade**, she decided to look for the bedroom to take a **petit** nap. In front of her, she saw a bed, but not just **un lit**, not just **deux lits**, but **trois lits**!

lit

Un, **deux**, **trois**! **Trois lits**! So, she tried the **lit** of the **papa ours**, but it was too **dur**. Then she tried the **lit** that belonged to the **maman**, but it was too **mou**.

Finally, she tried the **petit lit** of the **petit bébé ours** and said, "Ah. This one isn't too **dur**. It isn't too **mou**. It's just right!" And she fell asleep. At that very *moment*, the **ours** family returned from their **promenade**. But the **papa ours** noticed something strange. "Someone's been eating from my **bol**!" he said.

"And someone's been eating from my **bol**!" said the **maman**. "And someone's been eating from MY **bol** and ate everything up!" cried the **petit bébé ours**.

"Look!" said the **papa ours**. "Someone's been sitting in my **fauteuil**!" "And someone's been sitting in my **fauteuil**!"

said the **maman**. "And someone's been sitting in my **petit fauteuil** and broke it into little pieces!" cried the **petit bébé ours**.

Suddenly the **ours** family heard snoring coming from the bedroom so they went in to look. "Someone's been sleeping in my **lit**!" said the **papa ours**.

"And someone's been sleeping in my **lit**" said the **maman**. "And someone's been sleeping in MY **petit lit**... and there she is!" shouted the **petit bébé ours**.

Just then, Goldilocks woke up and was shocked to see the **ours** family! The **ours** family thought the young *fille* was very *méchante* to use their *maison*

without permission! "Oh, **merci**! **Merci** for letting me eat food from your **trois bols**, sit in your **trois fauteuils**, and lie in your **trois lits**!" Goldilocks

said "*Merci!*" again expecting the **ours** family to say, "*De rien!*" But they were angry that she caused so much trouble in their *maison* and the **ours** family growled at her.

So, she slowly stood up on the **petit lit** of the **petit bébé ours**, and said nervously, "Well, **merci** for having me. **Au revoir!**" And with that, Goldilocks jumped off the

29

petit lit, and dashed out the front **porte**, running as fast as each *pied* could move. Needless to say, she never returned to visit the *maison* of the **ours** family again.

Now you're ready for Level 3!

Level 3 contains words from Levels 1 & 2, plus all NEW words!

For more HEY WORDY! products, visit…

www.HEYWORDY!.com

www.ingramcontent.com/pod-product-compliance
Lightning Source LLC
Chambersburg PA
CBHW042031100526
44587CB00029B/4374